ESTEGOSAURIO

LUKE COLINS

BLACK
RABBIT
BOOKS

Bolt es una publicación de Black Rabbit Books
P.O. Box 3263, Mankato, Minnesota, 56002.
www.blackrabbitbooks.com
Copyright © 2021 Black Rabbit Books

Catherine Cates, diseñador del interior;
Grant Gould, diseñador de producción;
Omay Ayres, investigación fotográfica
Traducción de Travod, www.travod.com

Información del catálogo de publicaciones de la biblioteca del congreso
Names: Colins, Luke, author.
Title: Estegosaurio / por Luke Colins.
Other titles: Stegosaurus. Spanish
Description: Mankato, Minnesota : Black Rabbit Books, 2021. | Series: Bolt Jr.
Los dinosaurios | Includes index. | Audience: Ages 6-8 | Audience:
Grades K-1 | Summary: "Learn all about Stegosaurus through carefully
leveled text and easy-to-read infographics"— Provided by publisher.
Identifiers: LCCN 2019055498 (print) | LCCN 2019055499 (ebook) |
ISBN 9781623105426 (library binding) | ISBN 9781644664780 (paperback) |
ISBN 9781623105488 (ebook)
Subjects: LCSH: Stegosaurus—Juvenile literature.
Classification: LCC QE862.065 C6618 2021 (print) | LCC QE862.065 (ebook) |
DDC 567.915/3—dc23
LC record available at https://lccn.loc.gov/2019055498
LC ebook record available at https://lccn.loc.gov/2019055499

Impreso en los Estados Unidos de América

Créditos de las imágenes
Alamy: Amir Paz, 1; Stocktrek Images, Inc., Cover, 20–21; Universal Images Group
North America LLC / DeAgostini, 12–13; Dreamstime: Furzyk73, 6–7; Paleoguy:
James Kuether, 10–11; Science Source: JAIME CHIRINOS, 5; Mark Garlick, 18–19;
Shutterstock: aaabbbccc, 22–23; benntennsann, 3, 24; Dean zangirolami, 14–15;
Fundamentum, 6–7; Herschel Hoffmeyer, 8–9; I Wei Huang, 16–17; Johan
Swanepoel, 7; Valentyna Chukhlyebova, 4, 10, 13, 21

Contenido

En acción

Un estegosaurio come plantas silenciosamente. De repente, un carnívoro ataca. El estegosaurio intenta golpearlo con su cola con **púas**. ¡Cranch! El otro dinosaurio se escapa corriendo.

púas: puntas afiladas

Estegosaurio
9 a 12 pies
(3 a 4 metros)

COMPARACIÓN
DE ALTURAS

Un animal de gran tamaño

El estegosaurio era enorme. Crecía hasta alcanzar los 30 pies (9 m) de largo. Pesaba tanto como un coche. Grandes placas crecían en su espalda.

Estegosaurio

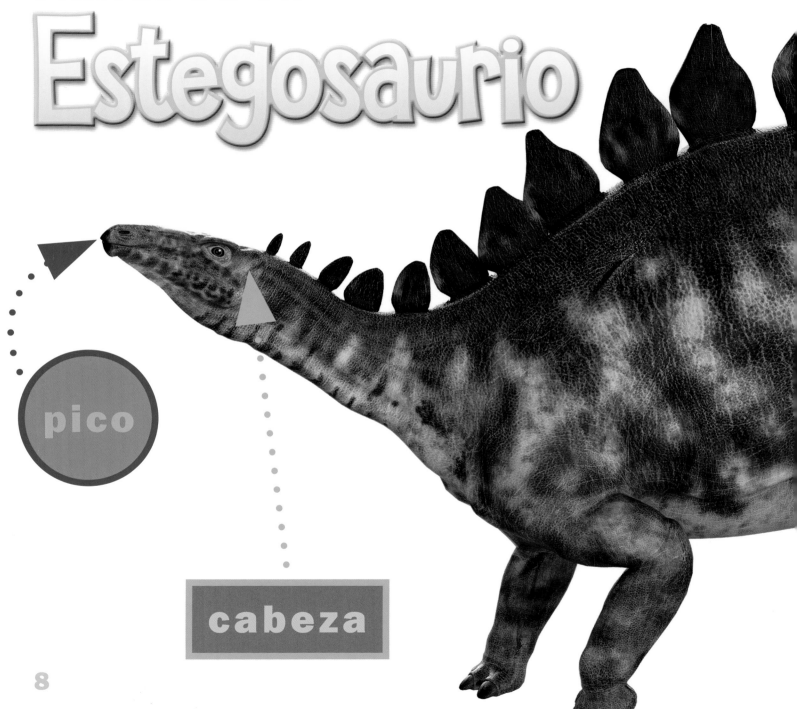

pico

cabeza

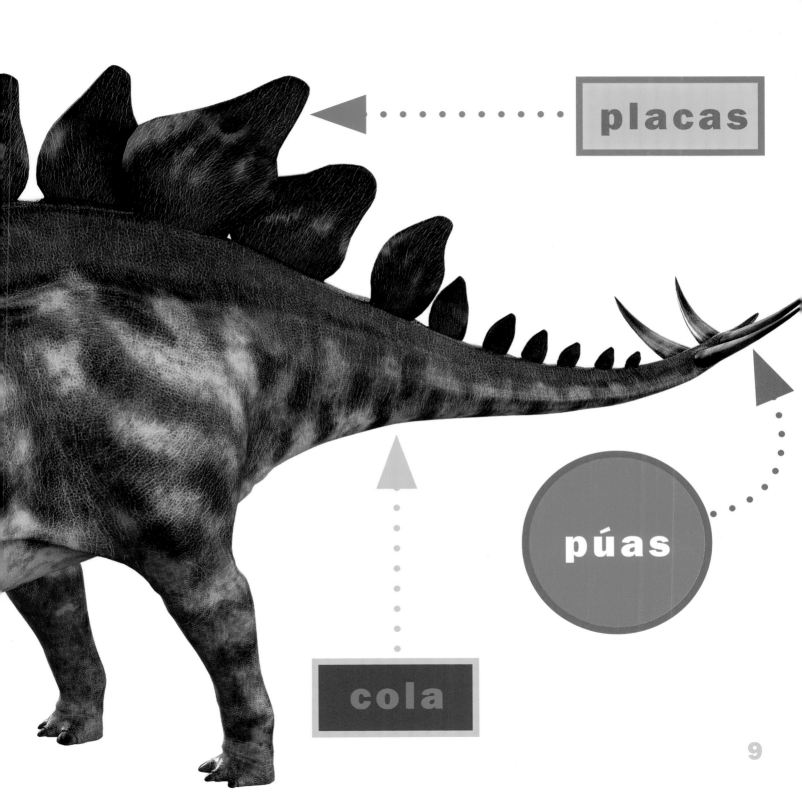

placas

púas

cola

La vida hace mucho tiempo

Estos dinosaurios vivieron hace unos 150 millones de años. Caminaban dando fuertes pisotones entre los **helechos**. Los científicos creen que vivían solos o en pequeños grupos.

helecho: un tipo de planta que tiene hojas grandes y no tiene flores

HECHO

El estegosaurio
tenía alrededor
de 78 dientes.

Alimentos

El estegosaurio comía principalmente plantas. Puede haber comido algunos **moluscos**. Era un animal de gran tamaño. Debía comer mucho cada día.

molusco: un animal que tiene una caparazón externa y vive en el agua

Donde se hallaron fósiles de estegosaurio

Wyoming

Utah

Colorado

Portugal

Al estudiarlos

Los científicos estudian los fósiles del dinosaurio. Quieren saber sobre su vida. Piensan que el estegosaurio podía morder con gran fuerza. Masticaba plantas muy duras.

HECHO

Algunas de sus placas medían 2 pies (1 m) de altura.

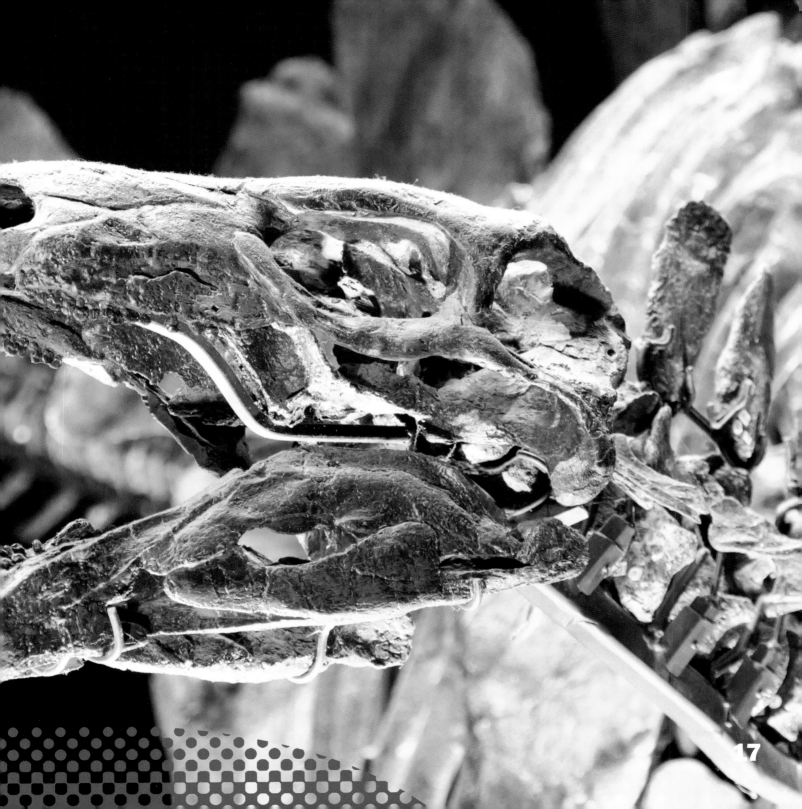

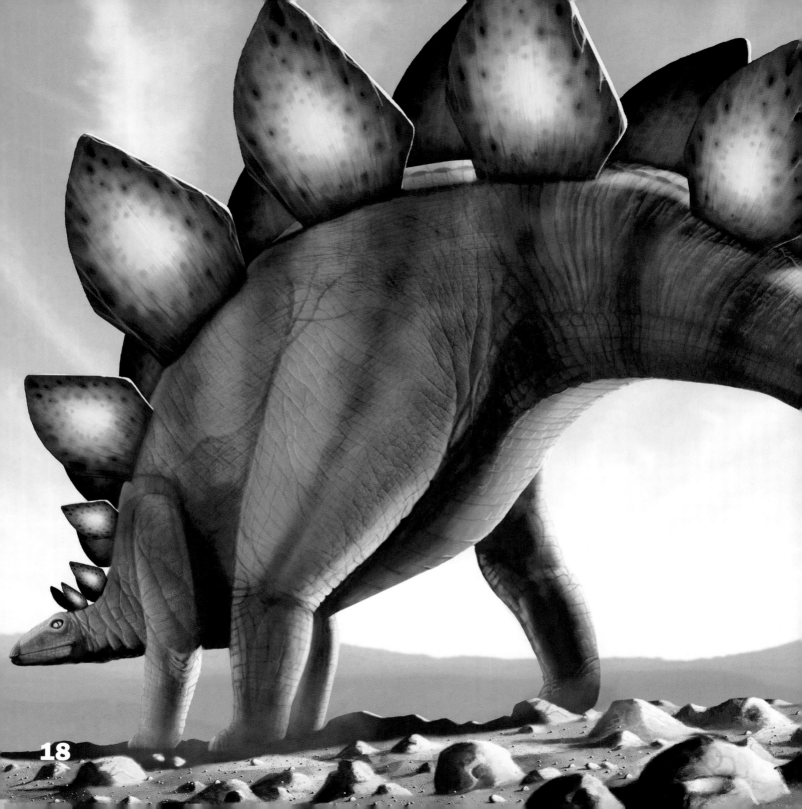

Al aprender

Los científicos también estudian
su cola. Piensan que usaba su cola
con púas para pelear.

La gente sigue buscando más fósiles.
Esperan poder aprender más
sobre este enorme animal.

púa de la cola
hasta **18** pulgadas
(46 centímetros) de largo

Información extra

Su nombre significa «lagarto con tejado».

Sus placas pueden haber sido coloridas.

Su cerebro era del tamaño de una lima.

El estegosaurio comía rocas para moler la comida en su estómago.

estómago: El lugar del cuerpo donde se mezcla la comida después de comer

21

GLOSARIO

estómago: el lugar del cuerpo donde se mezcla la comida después de comer

helecho: un tipo de planta que tiene hojas grandes y no tiene flores

molusco: un animal que tiene una caparazón externa y vive en el agua

púas: puntas afiladas

23

ÍNDICE

Acknowledgements

THERE ARE SO MANY PEOPLE TO THANK FOR THIS PROJECT. IT STARTS WITH LUANN KAPASI AND Steve Erwin from public affairs at Hôtel-Dieu Grace. Luann first contacted me more than a year ago to see if I'd be interested in pursuing a history of that institution. She opened a lot of doors for me in the process, setting up interviews, putting me in touch with so many individuals who knew the history better than I ever could. I worked closely with Toni Janik and Orien Duda, of the medical library and archives at Hôtel-Dieu Grace. The cooperation of this department, especially brought me great success. Through their efforts, most of the photographic or visual work in this book was unearthed from their files at Hôtel-Dieu. Rodney Carter of the Kingston archives for the Religious Hospitallers of St. Joseph also showed meticulous attention to my queries, and provided me with enormous resources that made my research so much easier. The Windsor Public Library staff on the second floor of the main branch was instrumental in helping me find the background to so many stories at Hôtel-Dieu Grace. Of course, without the help of Dr. Henri Breault's daughter, Rosemary, as well as Sisters Beaulieu, Dufault, LeBoeuf and so many others including Frank Bagatto, Bill Marra, Ken Deane, Frieda Parker Steele, Maria Giannotti and Barbara Porter this project would never have gotten off the ground. Assisting me in this research was Jessica Knapp, a former University of Windsor student of mine, and someone who was passionate about tracking down stories, files, photographs and checking and double-checking dates and statistical information. Her attention lifted a huge burden off my shoulders. Also aiding me in the last moments of this manuscript were Lisa Salfi, who, along with Brian Fox, edited this book, and Jay Rankin who handled all the photographic work. Karen Monck of Benchmark Publishing and Design shared her wisdom on the design, and gave me the reassurance to finish. I have to say, too, that without the encouragement of so many others, this history might not have been told. There was also the moral support that I received from the English Department at the University of Windsor, specifically Carol Davison, chair of that Department, as well as Cathy Masterson, Chris Menard, Roger Bryan, Peter Hrastovec, Mary Ann Mulhern, Karl Jirgens and Martin Deck. I must also thank my son, Stéphane Gervais, and my daughter-in-law Brenda for helping me with the French translations from the diaries of these francophone nuns. Top of the list of support, of course, is my wife Donna who let me slip away at the oddest hours so that I could finish this book. And to the wonderful staff at Tim Hortons at Ypres and Walker Road —they saw me coming at 4:30 a.m., and were ready with steeped tea and toasted bagels. I appreciated their interest in the progress of the book. They saw this is as my "office."

My thanks for the use and permission of photographs to: the *RHSJ Archives* (Windsor, Kingston); *Border Cities Star*, Canadian Medical Hall of Fame; Hôtel-Dieu Grace Hospital; Frieda Steele.

In the course of my research, the following need to be acknowledged (if I am missing anything, my apologies):

Neil F. Morrison's *Garden Gateway to Canada*; Annals of "The Sisters Hospitallers of the Hôtel-Dieu of St. Joseph of Windsor, Ontario"; *Annals* of The Religious Hospitallers of St. Joseph; *The Michigan Catholic*; Sister Cecile Comartin's *Our History of the Religious Hospitallers of St. Joseph, Windsor, Ontario*; Letters from Mother Pâquet to: Sandwich East Township, Hiram Walker & Sons, Mother Bonneau, T.F. Chamberlain of Toronto General Hospital (November 24, 1899), W.J. McKee (January 27, 1900); Letter from Bishop Michael Corrigan to Mother Pâquet; *The Evening Record*; Homily by Rev. M.P. Dowling, rector of Detroit College; *The Catholic Record* of London, Ontario; Father Wagner's Diary; Letter from Bishop Walsh to Father Wagner; Chapter 172 of the Revised Statutes of Ontario; *Dictionary of Canadian Biography*; Letter from Bishop O'Connor to The Sisters Hospitallers of the Hôtel-Dieu of St. Joseph of Windsor, Ontario; Annual Report of The Sisters Hospitallers of the Hôtel-Dieu of St. Joseph of Windsor, Ontario; Letter from Cyrilia to the Blessed Virgin on the occasion of her First Communion May 22, 1891; *The Quill: Jim McCollum*, Letter from "A Protestant who Doth Protest," Letter from Dr. Richard Carney, Letter from "Quo Warranto," Letter from "Citizen"; *The Evening Record*: Letter from "A Protesting Protestant," Letter from "A Protestant Ratepayer," Letter from The Home of the Friendless' Board of Management, Letter from Francis Cleary, Letter from William Kay (February 5, 1892), Letter from George Rankin (Colonel Rankin's son, March 20, 1893); October 30, 1890 editorial in French newspaper *Le Progress*;Biographers of Sister Sophie Lachapelle; Documents provided by the Religious Hospitallers of St. Joseph describing Sister Joséphine Pâquet; Biographer of Sister Joséphine Pâquet; Sister Comartin, biographer of Sister Joséphine Boucher; Biographer of Sister Philomène Carrière; Biographers of Sister Elizabeth Dupuis; Elder C.L. Morten; *Registre des Malades Du Monastere Des Religieuses Hospitalieres de St-Joseph et des Pauvres de Hôtel-Dieu*; Dr. Charles Casgrain; HLWIKI International's "History of Nursing in Canada"; *Ontario Water Quality, Public Health and the Law 1880-1930*, article by Jamie Benedickson; Advertisements by Pasteur Walter Filter by Morton & Christie; "The Cure of the Lame" in *The Religious Week* of Montreal; Results of the Crud Method; Testimonial of the mayor of Toulouse, France regarding the Crud Method (1899); Letters between Scully and A. Whiting on March 29, 1910, March 30, 1910, and April 4, 1910; Letter from Scully to Mother Guevin; *The Windsor Record*, 1907; August 24, 1907 Letter from medical staff sub-committee headed by Dr. J.S. LaBelle to Dr. Hoare, President of the Medical Staff Committee; Ada Vaughan's history of the Hôtel-Dieu School of Nursing: a thesis; *Record of Hôtel-Dieu of St. Joseph Hospital 1888-1928*; Michael Power's *Gather Up the Fragments: A History of the Diocese of London*; Biographers of Sister LaDauversiere; Archivists of Sister St. Charles at the Religious Hospitallers of St. Joseph; *The Kingston Whig*; Letter from Mother

Pâquet to Margaret A. Black, the Secretary to the Home of the Friendless, March 26, 1891; Letters between Sister Cecile Belleperche and Bishop Fallon between September 10, 1917 and November 7, 1917; Archives of the Religious Hospitallers of St. Joseph; Letters between Sister Marie de la Ferre and Bishop Fallon between August 1925 and January 1927; Letter from Bishop Fallon to the convent community on September 1, 1923; Letter from the sisters to Monsignor Di Maria on September 18, 1923; Nun's report of 1899; *The Windsor Star*; Letters between the Medical Staff Committee and The Sisters Hospitallers of the Hôtel-Dieu of St. Joseph of Windsor, Ontario between 1908 and 1920; Letter from E. Prouse from the Medical Staff Board to the Mother Superior on October 12, 1910; Letter from the Medical Staff Secretary to Sister St. Joseph; Letter from the Medical Staff Secretary to Bishop Fallon on January 23, 1922; George Siamandas' "The 1918 Influenza Outbreak: The Spanish Flu Panics Canada"; Review of Steven Palmer and Steve Malone's *Border City Medicine: Windsor's History of Innovative Health Practice*; *The Border Cities Star* headline "FLU' PATIENTS CROWD HOSPITAL; NO BEDS LEFT." Advertisement by The J. Gelber Furniture Company, November 11, 1918; Christopher Rutty and Sue C. Sullivan's *This is Public Health: A Canadian History*; *The Border Cities Star*; Article by C.C. Pierce in *The Boston Medical and Surgical Journal*; Stu Beitler's "Windsor, ON Detroit,

MI Tornado Leaves Ruin, Jun 1946"; Thomas Brophey's "First Eye-Witness Tells Graphic Story" in *The Windsor Star*; *The Windsor Daily Star*; Article by Chris Vander Doelen, July 1996 in *The Windsor Star*; "A Boy's Life," November 16, 2004, in the *Ottawa Citizen*; "The Present Outbreak of Poliomyelitis in Quebec" in *The Canadian Public Health Journal 23*, October 1932; Jane. S. Smith's *Patenting the Sun: Polio and the Salk Vaccine*; Peggy Bristow's "A Duty to the Past, A Promise to the Future: Black Organizing in Windsor" published in *The Journal of Black Canadian Studies* (New Dawn, Vol. 2, No. 1, 2007); "Cecile Wright Earns New Honors for Race" article in *Progress*; Notes of Sister Claire Maître; Biographers of Sister Claire Maître; Autobiographical notes by Sister Tétrault; Biographers of Sister Viola Beaulieu; Biographers of Sister Germaine Lafond; "I Was in Hell" article by Walter McCall, *The Windsor Star*; *The Star* interview of Roman Mann, 1988; 2012 interview of Rosemary Breault-Landry by Marty Gervais; *Clinical Toxicology* (1974); "Vision for the Future" discussion paper, 1991; Letter from Frank Bagatto to *The Windsor Star*, January 29, 1997; Doug Schmidt, *The Windsor Star*, 2002; Oral Presentation by Ken Deane; *Report of the Investigators of Surgical and Pathology Issues at Three Essex County Hospitals*.